Python Programming
For Kids

Complete Guide to Python

Programming for Kids

With Simple Projects &

Exercises To Get Started

Craig Berg

Your Gift

Let me help you master this and other programming languages quickly.

Visit

https://bit.ly/codetutorials

To Find Out More

Introduction

A computer has two main components: hardware and software. The hardware component of a computer refers to the parts of the computer that you can see and touch. Examples of computer hardware include the mouse, the keyboard, the monitor, etc.

On its part, the software component encompasses all the parts of the computer that you cannot touch; we normally refer to software as the interface you use to tell the computer what to do. Computers use the software and hardware components to do the things we want them to do.

Computers are not like people; they cannot do anything unless you 'program them.'

What is Programming?

Programming is the process of writing instructions that tell a computer what to do and how to do it. On the other hand, programmers are individuals who write instructions that tell the computer what to and how to do it.

Computers can do very many tasks such as playing music, doing homework, playing cool games, controlling a robot, creating movies and more. Computers can do these tasks because programmers have written instructions that tell the computer what to do.

What is a Program?

A program is a name we use to refer to the set of instructions written by a programmer to tell the computer what to do.

Programs are around you; they are in airplanes, cars, phones, refrigerators, toasters, and in a wide range of devices such as your PSP or handheld game console. When you play a game on the phone or in the arcade, it is thanks to a program written by a programmer.

For a programmer to write instructions or a program, he or she uses a tool called a programming language.

Programming Languages

Computers cannot understand our human languages. For us to tell them what to do, we use programming languages. Programming languages help us to write computer programs. There is a huge range of computer programming languages we can use to write computer programs. Each programming language can serve a different purpose.

The following are some of the popular programming languages and their primary use:

- ❖ **C:** Used to create complex software such as operating systems and embedded software for robots and machine learning

- ❖ **Java:** Used to create phone applications, computer applications, and some embedded software

- ❖ **JavaScript:** Used to create websites and web-based applications

- ❖ **MATLAB:** Used to perform mathematical operations and complex calculations

- ❖ **Python:** Used to create Windows applications, websites, and for data science.

In this guidebook, we shall be concentrating on Python programming language. Our primary aim shall be to learn how to simple Python programs. Along the way, we shall learn various things that will help you understand how to work with Python to create complex programs.

To start us off, let us discuss Python a bit deeply:

PS: I'd like your feedback. If you are happy with this book, please leave a review on Amazon.

Please leave a review for this book on Amazon by visiting the page below:

https://amzn.to/2VMR5qr

Table of Content

Part 1: Introduction to Python

How to Install Python and Create Your First Python Project/Program

Python is a snake, but in computing, it is not. In the computing world, Python is a high-level, interpreted computer programming language first created by Guido Van Rossum in 1989 who named the programming language as a tribute to a group of comedians known as "Monty Python."

We can use Python to create a wide range of programs, and in this book, we are going to learn everything we need to learn about Python so that we can be able to use it to write computer programs.

Why Python?

The following are some of the reasons why we are going to learn how to use Python to write programs—as opposed to using any other programming languages.

❖ **It is very beginner friendly:** Compared to other programming languages, Python is relatively easy to learn. It offers an interactive shell that allows you to enter programs and run them directly

❖ **Quick and efficient:** Python is a very clean and efficient programming language as it does not use complicated symbols such as dollar signs $, and hashes #

❖ **Amazing Modules:** Python has very good modules—we will learn how to use modules later—that help kids write good programs, which makes learning to program in Python fun and enjoyable

❖ **Cross Platform:** Python programs can run on most operating systems such as Mac OS, Windows, or Linux. If you write a Python program that can do division and run it on any devices, it will behave the same way

The other benefit of learning Python is that it is the most used programming language in fields such as animating, Artificial Intelligence, Data Science, Machine and Deep Learning.

To learn how to create Python programs, the first thing we need to do is install Python on our computer.

We are now going to look at how to do this:

How to Install Python on Your Computer

As mentioned, before we begin writing programs in Python, we need to install it on our computers. Out of the box, Python comes with all the tools you need to begin programming right away.

For this book, we are going to use Python 3, which at the time of writing this, is the updated and newer version of the python programming language.

How to Install Python on Windows

If you are running Windows on your computer, you can install Python by first opening your web browser and going to: https://www.python.org/downloads and selecting the latest version of python 3.

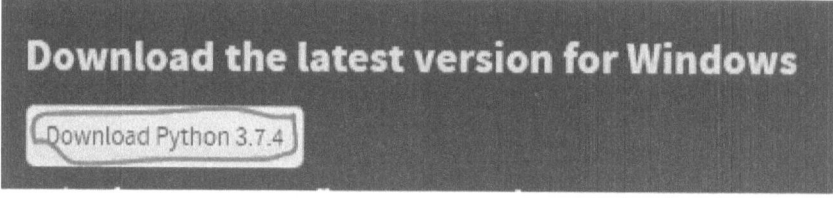

Once the python setup file has downloaded to your device, double click the installer icon to start installing Python on your computer. Follow the instructions given by the installer. Remember to note down the Python installation directory.

After successfully installing Python, you will notice a Python 3 entry in the Windows start menu. The version of python 3 we installed comes with a tool called **_Python IDLE shell._**

IDLE shell is an interactive, development and learning environment that allows us to write and test out python code, thus making it ideal for learning. IDLE shell provides an editor window that allows you to write your python code and save it so you can come back and use it later.

It also allows you to copy and paste text to and from other applications, thus reducing the amount of work required when writing python code. It also helps you format your python syntax—this means that it helps make sure that you write your python code in the correct way to avoid errors.

You can launch the Python IDLE by opening the Python 3 folders on your start menu and selecting IDLE (Python 4.7 32 bit).

How to Install Python on Mac

If you are using a Mac computer, open your browser and navigate to the following web page https://www.python.org/downloads/max-osx/ to download the installer for Mac OS just as we did for the Windows installer.

Make sure to select the correct version of your system.

Python Releases for Mac OS X

- Latest Python 3 Release - Python 3.7.4
- Latest Python 2 Release - Python 2.7.16

Stable Releases

- Python 3.7.4 - July 8, 2019
  - Download macOS 64-bit/32-bit installer
  - Download macOS 64-bit installer

Once the download completes, double-click on the installer you just downloaded and follow the instructions on the screen to install Python on your computer.

How to Install Python on Linux

If your computer is running a Linux-based system such as Ubuntu, Linux Mint, or Manjaro, the chances are high that you have Python already installed by default. However, the version installed may be an old version of the python programming language.

To install Python on Linux devices, you can launch the software center on the side bar. Once you have opened it, enter python 3 on the search bar, and then select the latest version of Python to begin installing.

How to Install Python on Android and iPhone

If you are using an android or an iPhone, you can still write Python code. To install Python for Android devices, open the Google Play Store and search for Pydroid 3 – IDE for Python. Once you find it, click Install to begin the installation process. For iPhone installation, open your Apple Store and search for Pythonista. This package is not open-source and you therefore have to pay $10 for the application.

Once you installed Python on your hardware, we can start writing python code.

How to Write Your First Python Program/Project

Now that you have installed Python on the device you are using, we can start creating our first python project. To do this, launch the IDLE; a window such as the one below shall display:

```
Python 3.7.4 Shell
File  Edit  Shell  Debug  Options  Window  Help
Python 3.7.4 (tags/v3.7.4:e09359112e, Jul  8 2019, 19:29:22) [MSC v.1916 32 bit
(Intel)] on win32
Type "help", "copyright", "credits" or "license()" for more information.
>>> |
                                                              Ln: 3  Col: 4
```

Once the IDLE has launched, it will tell you what version of Python you are using. It will also show you the current date and time. It also gives you the three greater than >>> signs called "the prompt." The prompt tells you that you can start entering your python code and run to see what it does.

We shall now write our first Python program using the Python IDLE. On the prompt, enter the following code making sure you include the double quotes.

```
print("Hi there, this is the computer")
```

Once you enter the code above, click the return/enter key to run your code.

What did you see?

Once you run the above code, the computer should respond with, "Hi there, this is the computer."

```
>>> print("Hi there, this is the computer")
Hi there, this is the computer
>>>
```

Congratulations: you just created your first Python program!

We use the above python code to print information—meaning displaying the required output on the screen—whatever text you enter between the double-quotes. As you can see, the computer does what you tell it to do, which in this case is displaying a sentence on the screen.

The result of your python code is called 'an output.' You should also note that the prompt reappears after printing out the result. Python is telling that it is ready to accept more commands.

Let us now save the python code we just created so that we can use it later. On the top menu of the Python IDLE, Click the option "File" and select Save. Now enter the name you would like to call the file. Now click save.

That is it: you have successfully created your first Python project/program.

Exercise 1

Now that we have covered how to write python code, go through the following multiple-choice questions that test out your understanding of what you just learned:

Question 1:

What is a Programming Language?

A. A fancy name for a dollar

B. A book for writing notes

C. A tool for telling the computer what to do to perform the tasks we want it to do

D. The physical part of a computer

Question 2:

In computing, what is Python?

A. A snake

B. A comedy group

C. A command

D. A programming language

Question 3:

What is Python IDLE?

A. An Integrated Development and Learning Environment

B. A word processor

C. A terminal

D. A text editor

Question 4:

What python command do you give a computer to print the words "My name is Bob?"

A. Println("My name is Bob")

B. Print – "My name is Bob"

C. print("My name is Bob")

D. print("My name is Bob)

Answers

The following are answer to the questions that make up exercise 1:

A. C

B. D

C. A

D. C

That was amazing work and you have learned a lot already!

Now that you have learned how to create your first Python program/project, we shall move on and start learning about important Python programming elements you need to know in order to start creating bigger and complex Python programs:

Part 2: Python Operators

How to Work With Python Operators

Now that we have already written our first program in Python, let us learn how to use Python to do some math. If mathematics is not your favorite cup of tea, do not worry; this is going to be the best part about learning how to program using Python: you will not have to do it on your own and shall instead teach your Python program how to solve mathematical problems.

First, what is 3 X 5? Your answer should be 15. Now, what is 126,546 X 45,004? This mathematical problem is not as easy to solve as the previous one—if you solved it, amazing work: you are great at math. If you could not solve this math problem, do not worry for we are going to learn how to use Python to complete these kinds of calculations for us.

Start the IDLE shell as we learned previously. Click on start, open the python folder and select IDLE.

Once you have launched the Python IDLE, enter the following 126546*45004. The * known as asterisk, is what the computer uses to perform multiplication. Now 'print' by hitting the return key to see the output. You will get an answer as shown in the following image:

```
Python 3.7.4 (tags/v3.7.4:e09359112e, Jul  8 2019, 19:29:22) [MSC v.1916 32 bit
(Intel)] on win32
Type "help", "copyright", "credits" or "license()" for more information.
>>> 125456 * 45004
5646021824
```

We can see that Python is able to perform mathematical calculations as we want it to. The asterisk we used above is an operator. In Python, we use operators to perform mathematical operations.

Here are the most common python operators:

Operator	Python	Human Beings
Addition	+	+
Subtraction	-	-
Multiplication	*	X
Division	/	.-.
Remainder	%	mod

Let us look at a realistic case.

Suppose you have a toy shop where you sell each toy at 35 dollars each, and you have a total of 600 toys. How much money would you make if you sold all the toys in one day? Let us find out in Python.

To get the total money you would make, take the total number of toys, and multiply that by the price of each toy. Python tells us that you would have made a total of 21000 dollars.

```
>>> 600 * 35
21000
>>> |
```

Now, from the total number of toys, let us assume that 100 of the toys malfunction before you sell them—hey, do not feel bad, this is part of business. How much money would you have made? To do this, take the total number of toys and subtract 100 then multiply by the price of each toy as shown below:

```
>>> 600-100*35
-2900
```

Python tells us that we would have made a loss of $2900. Do you think this correct? The answer is NO! It is correct to note that we had to subtract 100 from 600 to get the remaining toys before multiplying that number by the price of each toy.

Python sees this in a different way. It thinks that you want to multiply 100 by 35 dollars and then subtract 600 from that. This happens because every operator in Python has an order or precedence. Python performs division and multiplication before addition and subtraction. If Python encounters an operation that has more than one operator, it follows this order to do the calculations.

Another thing to note is that addition and subtraction has the same precedence and so does multiplication and division. If Python encounters a calculation with the different operators of the same precedence, it performs the calculation from left moving right.

Example:

9+9-3+6-2

If you run the above calculation in Python, it will give the following result:

```
>>> 9 + 9-3+6-2
19
```

This is true. Now let us look at another example with different operators.

Example: 1260 – 50 * 10 + 16 / 4

As we have seen, the precedence of division and multiplication comes before addition and subtraction. So Python will perform the calculation in the following order:

❖ First, multiply 50 * 10 = 100

❖ Second, divide 16 / 4 = 4

❖ Third, add all the values together as 1260 – 100 + 4 = 1164

Now you understand why your toy store ended up with you owing money to your toy distributor. What is the solution to the above problem?

To control how Python calculates our math, we use round brackets, also called as parenthesis (). We would like Python to first subtract the total number of spoilt toys from the total number of available toys.

For this, we put parenthesis around the calculation we would like Python to perform first. This means that in Python, a parenthesis has the highest precedence. In this case, we would type the calculation as: (600 − 100) * 35. Let us see what Python tells us:

```
>>> (600-100)*35
17500
```

Now you can see that you would make $17500 that day. Now that we have seen how to perform calculations with numbers, let us introduce a new concept.

Part 3: Python Variables

How to Work With Variables in Python

In the last part of the book, we looked at how much you could earn if you sold 600 toys in one day. What if in the next day, you only had 200 toys and the following day 100 toys? The total number of spoilt toys would also change every day. How would we calculate the total amount for each day? That is where variables come to help us.

What Are Variables?

You can think of variables as some sort of container where we can store the values we want. Imagine three containers, each with names as follows:

❖ toys_that_day

❖ toys_spoilt

❖ price_per_toy

In each of the containers, we can create any number we want to, remove the number we want, or add another number. In Python, each of these containers is what we call a variable.

In Python, we put the numbers we want using the equal sign (=). Therefore, if we want to tell Python to store the number 600 in the container – the variable in this case – toys_that_day, we do:

```
toys_that_day = 600
```

Now we can say that the total number of toys_that_day is 600. Now, to find out which value a variable or container holds, we use the print() command followed by the name of the variable in the parenthesis. Let us find out what value is stored in the toys_that_day variable: Type the following command:

```
toys_that_day = 600

print(toys_that_day)
```

```
>>> toys_that_day = 600
>>> print(toys_that_day)
600
```

Great, we get 600.

You may have noticed that we used underscores for the variable name instead of writing it as a sentence. When it comes to naming variables in Python, we have to follow certain rules so that Python does not get confused.

The rules that Python follow for naming a variable are as follows:

❖ Variable names can only consist of a letter, a number, or an underscore

❖ Variable names cannot contain any spaces or use special characters —special characters are characters that are not letters or numbers

❖ You can use underscores to separate words in a python variable

❖ You cannot start a variable name with a number or a special character

❖ Variable names are case sensitive —this means that a name such as Variable and variable, or vAriable and VariaBLE are not similar. Make sure you are careful about which letters are lower case or uppercase in the variable name

Another thing to note about variable names is you should try to name them as meaningful as possible. This will help you remember the values stored within a container. For example, if you want to store the total amount of money of a gaming console, you should name it something like price_of_xbox or price_of_ps4 instead of something such as console_money or ps4_buy.

Look at the following variable names and try to determine which one is correct in Python.

* ❖ Python.3

* ❖ 3python

* ❖ Python_3

* ❖ Python 3

The correct answer is C because, as we mentioned, a variable name cannot contain a special character (so remove A), it cannot start with a number (B is out) and a variable name cannot contain a space (D is out). Did you guess the answer correctly?

Now you know how to create and print variable names. Let us move on and see how to use variable names in Python. Let us first store a value in each of our variable names.

```
toys_that_day = 600

toys_spoilt = 100

price_per_toy = 35
```

Store the above values in their respective variable names in Python. It should be something like this:

```
>>> toys_that_day = 600
>>> toys_spoilt = 100
>>> price_per_toy = 35
```

Now instead of using numbers, we can perform our calculations using the variable names that store them. Let us try this in Python.

```
>>> (toys_that_day - toys_spoilt) * price_per_toy
17500
```

You can see that we get our earlier value of 17500 dollars. We can also store our earned money in its variable. Let us create a variable and call it money_earned_day1 = (toys_that_day – toys_spoilt) * price_per_day

```
>>> money_earned_day1 = (toys_that_day - toys_spoilt) * price_per_toy
>>> print(money_earned_day1)
17500
```

You can see that if we print the variable containing money earned that day, it gives us the previous value. What about if we wanted to do the same for the second day; what would we do?

In the second day, you had 200 toys and the total toys spoilt were 10. For this, you just make the variable for toys_that_day to hold 200 and the variable for toys_spoilt to hold 10. The price per toy remains the same. Using the earlier formula, we can create the money earned on the second day.

```
>>> toys_that_day = 200
>>> toys_spoilt = 10
>>> price_per_toy = 35
>>> money_earned_day2 = (toys_that_day - toys_spoilt) * price_per_toy
>>> money_earned_day2
6650
```

You can see we get 6650 dollars.

From this example, it is easy to see just how valuable and useful variables are in python programming. They allow us to create calculations as formulas that we can reuse by copying and pasting the code – only changing a few values.

Let us test out your knowledge of variable:

Exercise 2

Question 1:

Which of the following symbols represent division in Python?

A. –

B. +

C. *

D. /

E. All the Above

Question 2:

Which of the following names does not represent a valid Python variable name?

A. myfirstname

B. myFirstName2

C. my_First_name

D. Myfirst2name

E. @_2_myFirstname

Question 3:

What is the result of the following calculation in Python?

10 + (20-5) / 5 * 3

A. 27

B. – 7

C. 8

D. 6.5

E. 19

Question 4:

Which of the following is a valid python operator?

A. print()

B. add

C. div

D. *

E. Remainder

Answers

The answers to the second exercise are:

1. D

2. E

3. E

4. D

That was great work. In the next section, we are going to see more about variables. See you there.

Part 4: Strings and String Variables

How to Work With Strings and String Variables in Python

In the last part of the guide, we learned how to use Python variables to store numbers, the rules for creating a valid python variable, how to use python operators to do a calculation using variables, and how to display the numbers contained in the variable using python function print().

At this point, you may be wondering to yourself, is printing numbers the only use for variables? The answer is NO. Variables do more than just store numbers. We can also use them to store text.

In programming, we refer to text as string, which simply means a string of letters or characters. A string can contain any type of data. For example, a string can be a number, a name, an address, a country, etc. If a variable is holding a string, we call it a string variable.

Do you remember the first python project we worked on? We printed the words "Hi there, this is the computer." This is a string of text.

We enclose the text in double or single quotes to let Python know that we are creating a string. This helps Python not to confuse your string with its own words like print. We cannot create string variables as normal variables as we did with numbers; doing this will return a syntax error.

```
my_string = Hi there
```

```
>>> my_string = Hi there
SyntaxError: invalid syntax
```

If you get a syntax error, Python is simply telling you that you made a mistake in the arrangement of words and symbols in the given command. This makes the difference between number values and string values in Python.

In Python, we always enclose string values in double quotes or single quotes. In Python, every command given must follow rules known as syntax; otherwise, Python will not understand what to do.

Let us now try to create a string variable called hello and let it store the string "Hello World" and print it.

```
>>> hello = "Hello world"
>>> print(hello)
Hello world
```

From the above example, we have enclosed the string in double quotes at the start and at the end. In Python, if you start a string with a double quote, you should make sure you end with a double quote. The same case applies for single quotes. Do not mix single and double quotes.

```
>>> double_quotes = "Hello world"
>>> double_quotes = 'Hello world'
```

Now let us try writing the string 'I love python' and intentionally leave out the closing bracket as shown below:

```
>>> my_string = 'I love python
SyntaxError: EOL while scanning string literal
>>>
```

This time, Python returns a syntax error with a description as – 'EOL while scanning string literal'. This means that Python is expecting something before ending the line. That is why it returned the error with End of Line (EOL).

Now, let us try changing the my_string to hold the string 'This is dad's computer' and try printing it out.

```
>>> my_string = 'This is dad's computer'
SyntaxError: invalid syntax
```

Why did Python return an error? When Python sees the single quotes after 'dad', it automatically thinks that this is the end of your string and gets confused to get other commands it does not understand.

The solution to this problem is twofold:

❖ Using a single quote where a double quote is required. For example, when using direct speech, we use single quotes as shown below:

```
>>> peter = 'He said "I love Programming".'
>>> print(peter)
He said "I love Programming".
```

However, this will not always work as you may encounter other single quotes inside the double quotes.

❖ Using escape characters: Escape characters are characters that help us to use the quotation marks we want in our string. Python uses "\" character as an escape character; for example:

```
>>> my_string = 'This is dad\'s computer.'
>>> print(my_string)
This is dad's computer.
```

Again, a problem may rise when we want to use multiple lines. Let us say you want to create a story about your house. This would expand to multiple lines of your code. A string that expands to more than one line is a *multi-line string*. If you try to enter this kind of string in Python, it will treat the next lines as the next commands. Since the sentence will not be making any sense to Python, it will give an error.

Let us try it:

```
>>> my_house = "My house is in Hannah, South Carolina, USA. It is a quite new ho
use. It was built only one year back. It has two storeys".
SyntaxError: invalid syntax
```

In order to avoid these kinds of problems, we start and end a multi-line string with three double quotes """   """.

Let us try the above example again:

```
>>> my_house = """My house is in Hannah, South Carolina, USA. It is a quite new
house. It was built only one year back. It has two storeys"""
>>> print(my_house)
My house is in Hannah, South Carolina, USA. It is a quite new house. It was buil
t only one year back. It has two storeys
```

Strings with Values

Now that we have covered single and multi-line string values, let us move on to something new: string embedding. Do not let the new vocabulary scare you; we shall explain what it is.

Say you want to print a message that contains a value of another variable. For example, you have a variable called age and you want to add it to the value of another variable called about_bob. Now, about_bob variable holds the sentence that tells you how old Bob is. For this case, we use a placeholder – a value set for use in the place of another value.

Let us see an example:

```
>>> age = 12
>>> about_bob = "Bob is %s years old"
```

Look at the second line. We use a placeholder, %s – known as modulus s– to let Python know that is the place where we will insert the value of another variable. To print the age, we can do:

```
>>> age = 12
>>> about_bob = "Bob is %s years old"
>>> print(about_bob %age)
Bob is 12 years old
```

In the third line, we are telling Python to replace the %s, with the value of the variable of Bob's age. We can use placeholders to represent both strings and numbers. Let us do a quick simple quiz.

Calculate how old Bob will be in 10 and 15 years and display the result:

To do this, we declare the current age of Bob, age of Bob after 10 years, and age of Bob after 15 years. We can then use placeholder to display the ages. For example:

```
>>> current_age = 12
>>> after_ten_years = current_age + 10
>>> after_fifteen_years = after_ten_years + 5
>>> print("Bob will be %s years old after 10 years"%after_ten_years)
Bob will be 22 years old after 10 years
>>> print("Bob will be %s years old after 15 years"%after_fifteen_years)
Bob will be 27 years old after 15 years
```

Now Python tells us that Bob will be 22 years old after 10 years and 27 years old after 15 years.

Exercise 3

Take the following quick exercise that tests your understanding of everything we have learned about strings and string variables.

Question 1:

Write a python program that contains three variables. The first variable holds your first name, the second holds your last name, and the other holds your current age. Now create a string variable that prints your full name and age together in one string. For example, "Bob Fisher is 12 years old."

Question2:

Write a python program that calculates how many hours of homework you do in one week if you do 2 hours every weekday and 1 hour on weekends. The program should also contain a variable called *name*.

Question 3:

Write a python code that prints the sentence enclosed within the brackets.

```
(Shouldn't, couldn't, wouldn't are words you
shouldn't write in school) - ignore the brackets.
```

NOTE: use a single quote to start and end the string.

Example Solutions:

Question 1

```
>>> first_name = "Bob"
>>> last_name = "Fisher"
>>> age = 12
>>> all_information = "%s %s is %s years old"
>>> print(all_information%(first_name, last_name,age))
Bob Fisher is 12 years old
```

Great work! We used placeholders to hold the value of variables: first_name, last_name and age. On the print statement, Python inserted the appropriate variable values whenever it came across a placeholder one after the other.

Question 2

```
>>> weekdays = 5
>>> weekends = 2
>>> weekdays_work = 5 * 2
>>> weekends_work = 2 * 1
>>> total_hours = weekdays_work + weekends_work
>>> print("I do my homework for %s hours "%(total_hours))
I do my homework for 12 hours
```

Question 3

```
>>> words_not_to_write = 'shouldn\'t couldn\'t wouldn\'t are words you shouldn\'t write in school'
>>> print(words_not_to_write)
shouldn't couldn't wouldn't are words you shouldn't write in school
```

Part 5: Python Lists

Working with Python Lists

The last part of the guide gave us a good idea of how to work with strings and string variables. From that section, we now know that a string can store both strings and numbers. We also know how to print single-lined as well as multi-line strings. We can also comfortably use placeholders in Python.

In the previous chapter, we discussed how to calculate a person's age after a certain number of years. Did you notice that we had to include many variables when printing out someone's age?

Imagine we have 10 friends whose age in the next 10 years we want to calculate. It would be tiresome because it would require us to write a lot of code. Luckily, Python has the functionality of using lists to get around this problem. Let us see what Python lists do, shall we?

What are Python Lists

Python lists allow us to store a range of strings and numbers values in just one variable. Lists also give us the ability to organize these values in a way that allows us to use each part of the list individually whenever we need it.

Let us introduce all our 10 friends to Python—I hope you have that many friends☺.

```
>>> my_friends = ["Ruby","James","Emma","Potter","Lisa", "Alex","Ann","Robert","Riley","Hermione"]
>>> print(my_friends)
['Ruby', 'James', 'Emma', 'Potter', 'Lisa', 'Alex', 'Ann', 'Robert', 'Riley', 'Hermione']
```

This is how we assign strings to a list variable: We use square brackets [ ] to tell Python that what we are creating is a list variable. We also separate each string with a comma — otherwise Python will give us an error. Once we print it out, we get the list of our friends.

We can also refer to each item in a python list by using indexes. For example, if we want to refer to our friend Potter —who is in the fourth position in the friend's list— we would say: my_friends[3]. The reason we set the friend's position as zero is because Python counts from position zero as follows:

Friend	Index/position
Ruby	0
James	1
Emma	2
Potter	3
Lisa	4
Alex	5
Ann	6
Robert	7
Riley	8
Hermione	9

As we can see, Ruby has an index of 0, James has an index of 1, Emma has an index of 2 and so on such that our friend Potter is at index 3. Let us try this in Python:

```
>>> print(my_friends[3])
Potter
>>>
```

You can see that it printed out Potter. Now let us do a quick challenge. On your own, create a list called friends_ages and store the value of our friend's ages in the correct order. Now try to determine the age of three friends in the next 10 years.

Did you get it right?

Let us see how you would approach such a problem. First, let us create a list containing our friend's ages.

```
>>> friends_ages = [12,14,13,12,11,10,17,19,16,13]
```

Let us pick one friend and calculate their age in the next 10 years. Let us pick Hermione.

```
>>> print('In 10 years, %s will be %s years old'%(my_friends[9],friends_ages[9]+10))
In 10 years, Hermione will be 23 years old
```

Python tells us that Hermione will be 23 years old in the next 10 years. This is because Hermione is the last item in the list at index 9. Since we want her age after 10 years, we add 10 years to the value of her current age.

Do not get lost. The first line gets her name by referencing my_friends[9] and then getting her age by calling friends_ages[9] and then adding 10 – this gives us 13 + 10.

On your own, calculate the age of the following friends in the next 15 years: Potter, James, and Riley.

The best part of using lists is that you can easily replace the values in a list by using its index. For example, let us say we are no longer friends with James and have made a new friend called Ken. All we must do is to use James' index to replace both his name and his age values.

```
>>> my_friends[1] = "Ken"
>>> friends_ages[1] = 15
>>> print(my_friends)
['Ruby', 'Ken', 'Emma', 'Potter', 'Lisa', 'Alex', 'Ann', 'Robert', 'Riley', 'Hermione']
```

You can see that we replaced James with our new friend, Ken –James was a good friend though☺.

We can also add two lists in one list. For example, we can combine both names and ages of our friends into a single list. For example:

```
>>> names_and_ages = [my_friends,friends_ages]
>>> print(names_and_ages)
[['Ruby', 'Ken', 'Emma', 'Potter', 'Lisa', 'Alex', 'Ann', 'Robert', 'Riley', 'Hermione'], [12, 15, 13, 12, 11, 10, 17, 19, 16, 13]]
>>>
```

The third list, names_and_ages will only have two items – my_friends and friends_ages. This is because it consists of two list variables and not the contents of the variables. If you want to get Ken's name, you cannot enter names_and_ages[1] – this will give you a whole list of the friends ages since the list variable friends_ages is in index 1 of the list variable names_and_ages. Example:

```
>>> names_and_ages[1]
[12, 15, 13, 12, 11, 10, 17, 19, 16, 13]
```

To refer to Ken's name, we refer to the first list in the first square bracket and then the index of Ken's name in the second bracket. For example:

```
>>> print(names_and_ages[0][1])
Ken
```

This returns Ken's name. The first square bracket is referring to the first element in the list, which is the entire friends' names; the second square bracket is referring to the second item in the friend's names list.

Let us say we make new friends Sarah and Michael. To add values to an existing list, we use the .append() function —a function is a piece of code that tells Python to perform a specific task.

We will discuss more about functions later –for now, just know that we use the append() function to add items to a list. To add Sarah and Michael to the my_friends list, we do:

```
>>> my_friends.append("Sarah")
>>> my_friends.append("Michael")
>>> print(my_friends)
['Ruby', 'Ken', 'Emma', 'Potter', 'Lisa', 'Alex', 'Ann', 'Robert', 'Riley', 'Hermione', 'Sarah', 'Michael']
```

We refer to the list we want to add to and then call the append() function passing the item we want to add. In this case: my_friends.append("friend name")

Suppose we find out that becoming friends with Sarah and Michael was not a good idea. We can remove them from the list using the del command – yes, we said a command instead of function. We always close a function with parenthesis while a command does not.

Let us see an example:

```
>>> del my_friends[10]
>>> del my_friends[10]
>>> print(my_friends)
['Ruby', 'Ken', 'Emma', 'Potter', 'Lisa', 'Alex', 'Ann', 'Robert', 'Riley', 'Hermione']
```

We use the del command, followed by the index of the value we want to remove. You may notice that we used index 10 twice – this is because once the first command executes, it removes the item on index 10 and pushes forward the item in index 11 to occupy the empty index. This makes the previous index 11 to become index 10.

Exercise 4

Quiz Time again. This exercise may be a bit challenging, but you are up to the task☺:

Question 1

Write a python program that contains three lists. The first list contains the names of five of your friends, the second list holds their ages, and the third list holds their favorite video games. Using five separate commands, print five lines with the following format. "Hermione, who's 13 years old, loves to play Battlestar Galactica".

Question 2

Write a program that contains five of your best hobbies. Remove the second hobby from the list and then print the remaining hobbies.

Question 3

Write a program that contains a list of the top 10 destinations you would like to visit. Next, add, Padar Island and Kyoto.

Finally, delete these two destinations after you have visited them.

Question 4

Write a program containing three lists. The first list contains five American states' names, the second list contains their corresponding abbreviations, and the third contains a list of the first and the second list. Next, add a new state name and its corresponding abbreviation and print it out.

Example Solutions

Here are some sample solutions for the above exercises

Solution 1

```
>>> my_friends = ["Ruby","Ken","Emma","Potter","Hermione"]
>>> ages = [11,10,12,11,16]
>>> fav_games = ["Overwatch","Fortnite","Minecraft","Grand Theft Auto","Battlestar Galactica"]
>>> print("%s who\'s %s years old loves to play %s"%(my_friends[0],ages[0],fav_games[0]))
Ruby who's 11 years old loves to play Overwatch
>>> print("%s who\'s %s years old loves to play %s"%(my_friends[1],ages[1],fav_games[1]))
Ken who's 10 years old loves to play Fortnite
>>> print("%s who\'s %s years old loves to play %s"%(my_friends[2],ages[2],fav_games[2]))
Emma who's 12 years old loves to play Minecraft
>>> print("%s who\'s %s years old loves to play %s"%(my_friends[3],ages[3],fav_games[3]))
Potter who's 11 years old loves to play Grand Theft Auto
>>> print("%s who\'s %s years old loves to play %s"%(my_friends[4],ages[4],fav_games[4]))
Hermione who's 16 years old loves to play Battlestar Galactica
```

Solution 2

```
>>> my_hobbies = ["Comic Books","Video Games","Origami","Chess","Computer Pgrogramming"]
>>> del my_hobbies[1]
>>> print(my_hobbies)
['Comic Books', 'Origami', 'Chess', 'Computer Pgrogramming']
```

Solution 3

```
>>> rav_destinations = ["Sydney Opera House","Times Square","Rock Mts","Bora Bora","Queenstown"]
>>> fav_destinations.append("Padar")
>>> fav_destinations.append("Koyto")

>>> del rav_destinations[6]
>>> del fav_destinations[5]
>>> print(fav_destinations)
['Sydney Opera House', 'Times Square', 'Rock Mts', 'Bora Bora', 'Queenstown']
```

Solution 4

```
>>> states = ["Texas","Utah","Oregon","South Carolina","Virginia"]
>>> state_codes = ["TX","UT","OR","SC","VA"]
>>> all_info = [states,state_codes]
>>> print(all_info)
[['Texas', 'Utah', 'Oregon', 'South Carolina', 'Virginia'], ['TX', 'UT', 'OR', 'SC', 'VA']]
>>> all_info[0].append("Massachusetts")
>>> all_info[1].append("MA")
>>> print(all_info)
[['Texas', 'Utah', 'Oregon', 'South Carolina', 'Virginia', 'Massachusetts'], ['TX', 'UT', 'OR', 'SC', 'VA', 'MA']]
```

Now that you know how to use lists, let us move on to the next section:

Part 6: Tuples and Dictionaries

Working With Tuples and Dictionaries in Python

At this point, we have learned how to use strings and numbers into lists, how to add items to a list, how to delete items in a list, how to change individual items in a list, and finally, how to add lists in another list —also called nested lists.

Now, there are other ways to organize sets of strings in Python called Tuples and dictionaries. Let us discuss these two python elements to see how they work.

What are Tuples

Tuples are like list in the way they are organized. They contain a fixed set of items. However, you cannot delete, change, or add to the items and their values in a tuple.

In programming, this aspect of items being unchangeable is a phenomenon called immutability. This means that unlike lists, tuples are immutable —because you cannot change them. You are probably wondering why you would want to use a fixed item.

We use tuples in instances where we have some sets of values we would not want to change. For example days of the week or months in a year —we all know that months will always be the same and in the same order, unless you move to Mars. Another example of values you would want to use tuples for are the Fibonacci Series, mathematical formulas, etc.

To define a tuple in Python, we use the parenthesis instead of the square brackets we previously used for lists. For example:

```
>>> all_days = ("Sunday","Monday","Tuesday","Wednesday","Thursday","Friday","Saturday")
```

Again, if we want to refer to an individual item in the tuple, we use the same indexing format as in Lists. For example, to select Saturday – which is at index 6– we enter the command:

```
>>> print(all_days[6])
Saturday
```

REMEMBER: The indexing of items in both Lists and Tuples starts at 0. Simply put, the index is one number less than the position of your item – so the index of item number 100 is: $100 - 1 = 99$

What are Dictionaries

Dictionaries, also called Maps or dicts, are just a collection of Lists or Tuples. They offer a lot of flexibility in how we store our values – we will talk about this later. Dictionaries consist of keys and a corresponding value. Do you remember the age problem we solved earlier? It was pretty messed up, right?

We can solve the same problem in a more organized way where we store our friends' names, ages, and their games in one variable. In fact, there is nothing wrong with using nested lists like names_and_ages variable we created, but what if you had over 200 friends? You would need to calculate the index of the friend you want each time – which can be very tiresome.

Let us look at how we create dictionaries in Python – Pay attention to the syntax because it is very important. It may look scary though.

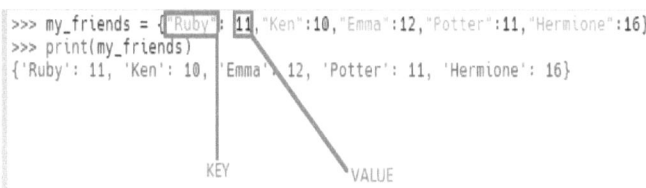

```
>>> my_friends = {"Ruby":11,"Ken":10,"Emma":12,"Potter":11,"Hermione":16}
>>> print(my_friends)
{'Ruby': 11, 'Ken': 10, 'Emma': 12, 'Potter': 11, 'Hermione': 16}
```

                    KEY   VALUE

Here, we are telling Python to create a dictionary with a friend's name and their corresponding age. If we want to get the age of one of the friend's, we just need to remember their name —who can forget a friend's name. For example, to print the age of Hermione:

```
>>> print(my_friends["Hermione"])
16
```

Let us take another example.

Suppose we want to perform each specific task on a specific day. We can use tuples and dictionaries to join/merge the two. For example, check out our daily routine below.

Day	Routine
Sunday	Snowboarding
Monday	Chess
Tuesday	Baking
Wednesday	Badminton
Thursday	Cycling
Friday	Swimming
Saturday	Rock climbing

We have already defined the days of the week as a tuple. Also remember that we used all_days[index] to get the day we want. We can also use the system technique to define each value for the key. For example:

```
>>> daily_routine = {all_days[0]:"Snowboarding",all_days[1]:"Chess",all_days[2]:"Baking",all_days[3]:"Badminton",
all_days[4]:"Cycling",all_days[5]:"Swimming",all_days[6]:"Rock Climbing"}
>>> print(daily_routine)
{'Sunday': 'Snowboarding', 'Monday': 'Chess', 'Tuesday': 'Baking', 'Wednesday': 'Badminton', 'Thursday': 'Cycling
', 'Friday': 'Swimming', 'Saturday': 'Rock Climbing'}
```

Python stored the days of the week as the dictionary keys while the activities we do will be the values. We can also create a tuple and use it to store the activities and just refer to their indexes. Now, what day is today? Try finding out which activity you should be doing.

```
>>> print(daily_routine["Monday"])
Chess
```

Looks like today is Chess day.

Let us take an example where you want to clear a day's activity – Saturday is always free. We can delete items in a dictionary by using the key of the item. Simply put, a dictionary key acts as the index for the element. For example, to clear our activity on Saturday, we use:

```
>>> del daily_routine["Saturday"]
>>> print(daily_routine)
{'Sunday': 'Snowboarding', 'Monday': 'Chess', 'Tuesday': 'Baking', 'Wednesday': 'Badminton', 'Thursday': 'Cycling', 'Friday': 'Swimming'}
```

Finally, assume an instance where we decide that Cycling on Thursday does not work for us and instead we want to do Kayaking. We can update the value by simply referring to its key as show:

```
>>> print(daily_routine)
{'Sunday': 'Snowboarding', 'Monday': 'Chess', 'Tuesday': 'Baking', 'Wednesday': 'Badminton', 'Thursday': 'Cycling', 'Friday': 'Swimming'}
>>> daily_routine["Thursday"] = "Kayaking"
>>> print(daily_routine)
{'Sunday': 'Snowboarding', 'Monday': 'Chess', 'Tuesday': 'Baking', 'Wednesday': 'Badminton', 'Thursday': 'Kayaking', 'Friday': 'Swimming'}
```

The best thing about dictionaries is that it automatically updates the corresponding index. For example, when we deleted the Saturday's activity, it automatically updated the index of Wednesday.

Exercise 5

Quiz time. Get ready because it is about to get more challenging –but you can handle it!

Question 1

Write a program that contains a tuple called "months" that holds the twelve months of the year in the consecutive order and a dictionary that holds the name of your 5 favorite friends as the keys and their month of birth. Print the month of birth of your two friends. For example, "Ruby was born on September"

Question 2

From the map you created, delete one of your friends and the print out the map to see if it deleted successfully.

Question 3

Create a dictionary called "my_dict" that contains the following words and their meanings. The words should be the keys and their definitions as the values.

❖ Chemistry – "the study of form and functions of basic elements"

❖ Python – A large non-venomous snake

❖ Dictionary – a book to lookup the meaning of words

❖ Pet – a domestic or tames animal

Now, print the meaning of the word "Dictionary" and then change it to "A python element for storing values flexibly." Finally, print out the entire dictionary to see if you got it right.

Question 4:

Which of the following are true for python dictionaries?

A. They contain a key and a value

B. They are created with parenthesis

C. They are immutable

D. Dictionary keys cannot be used as indexes

Question 5

Which of the following is a valid python dictionary?

A. Names = ({"name": "Python"})

B. Name = [("name": "Python")]

C. Name = {"name": "Python"}

D. Name = {"name": "Python"]

Example Solutions

Example solutions for Exercise 4

Solution 1

```
>>> months = ("January","February","March","April","May","June","July","August","September","October","November","December")
>>> friends = {"Ruby":months[8],"Emma":months[2],"Ken":months[6],"Hermione":months[10],"Potter":months[5]}
>>> print("Ruby was born %s"%friends["Ruby"])
Ruby was born September
>>> print("Emma was born in %s"%friends["Emma"])
Emma was born in March
```

Solution 2

```
>>> del friends["Ruby"]
>>> print(friends)
{'Emma': 'March', 'Ken': 'July', 'Hermione': 'November', 'Potter': 'June'}
```

Solution 3

```
>>> my_dict = {"Chemistry":"the study of form and functions of basic elements","Python":"A large non-venomous snake","Dictionary":"a book to lookup the meaning of words","Pet":"a domestic or tamed animal"}
>>> print(my_dict["Dictionary"])
a book to lookup the meaning of words
>>> my_dict["Dictionary"] = "A python element for storing values flexibly"
>>> my_dict
{'Chemistry': 'the study of form and functions of basic elements', 'Python': 'A large non-venomous snake', 'Dictionary': 'A python element for storing values flexibly', 'Pet': 'a domestic or tamed animal'}
```

Solution 4

1. A

Solution 5

1. D

As you can see, working with tuples and dictionaries in Python is relatively easy and all you really need to do is practice −a lot.

Let us move on to the next part:

Part 6: Turtle Graphics

Working With Python Turtle Graphics

Congratulations! At this point in the guide, you know the fundamental building blocks of the python programming language. You know about numbers, strings, lists, tuples, and dictionaries.

In this part of the guide, we shall look at something fun: drawing with python turtle.

What is Turtle

Turtle is a very handy Python tool. It is a module —we shall discuss what a module later— that helps us draw in Python.

Before we can use the turtle module, we need to import it. To import a module into Python, we use import <module name>

```
>>> import turtle
>>>
```

It looks like nothing happened; this is a good thing since we did not get an error. For example, if you try to import a module that does not exist, Python will return an error as shown below:

```
>>> import unknown_module
Traceback (most recent call last):
  File "<pyshell#2>", line 1, in <module>
    import unknown_module
ModuleNotFoundError: No module named 'unknown_module'
```

Now that we have imported Turtle, let us learn how to start using the turtle module. The first step is to create a drawing canvas where we shall do all our drawing. To create a canvas, simply use the pen() function.

```
>>> t = turtle.pen()
```

This will display a blank window with an arrow at the center. This window is what we call a canvas:

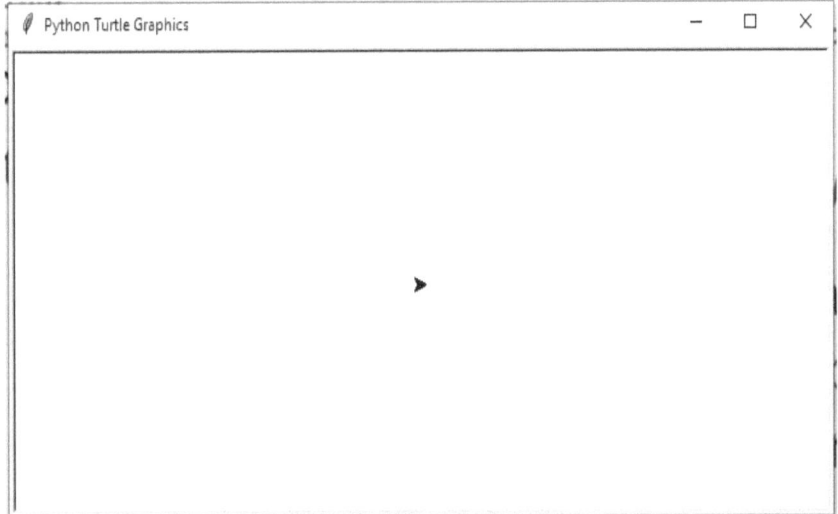

The arrow in the center is the turtle – although it does not look like a turtle. Now let us make the turtle move and draw as it moves.

The basic movements for the python turtle are; move forward, move backwards, turn left and turn right by various degrees. Let us make our turtle to move forward. We can do this by calling t.turtle() function. For example:

```
>>> t = turtle.Pen( )
>>> t.forward(50)
```

From the above command, we tell Python to make t, which in this case refers to the turtle, to move forward by 50 pixels or by 50 points. In a computer, a pixel is the smallest point on the computer screen –your computer screen consists of very tiny dots called as pixels. This is an example of a highly magnified number on a computer screen.

So the python turtle moves forward while drawing. Let us make it go to the left using t.left() function.

```
>>> t.left(90)
```

This tells the turtle to move left by 90 degrees. Now, if we want the turtle to turn right, we just change it to right(90). The diagram below shows which directions the turtle will take after angle variations.

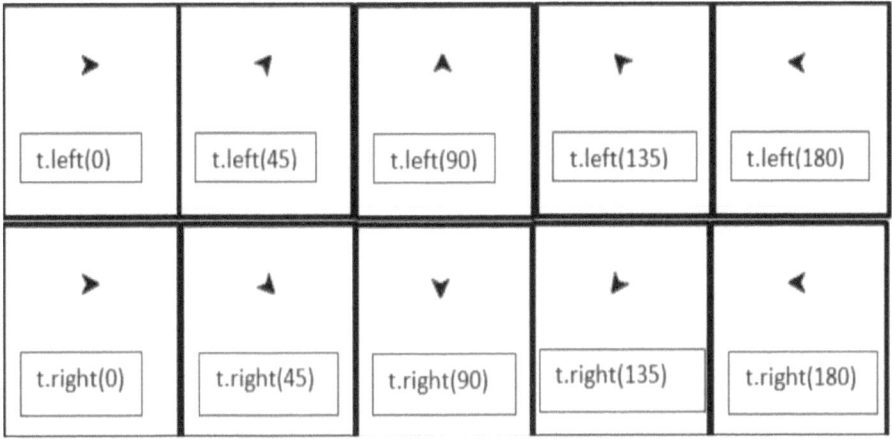

t.left(0)	t.left(45)	t.left(90)	t.left(135)	t.left(180)
t.right(0)	t.right(45)	t.right(90)	t.right(135)	t.right(180)

This time, let us make the turtle move 50 pixels forward in the left direction. For example:

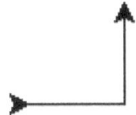

This time, the turtle moves 50 pixels left to the left. Try completing the diagram by making a square. Did you manage to create the square – let us see how to create it.

```
>>> import turtle
>>> t = turtle.Pen()
>>> t.forward(50)
>>> t.left(90)
>>> t.forward(50)
>>> t.left(90)
>>> t.forward(50)
>>> t.left(90)
>>> t.forward(50)
```

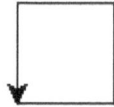

Let us learn some more. Let us try a new function to see what happens.

```
>>> t.reset()
>>>
```

Now, look at the turtle graphic – Where did our Square go?

We use the turtle reset() function to tell Python to delete everything created by the turtle module –quite damaging if you use it wrongly. You can also see that the turtle arrow returned to the default location. The reset function differs from the clear() function that does the same operation leaving the turtle at the current position. Let us see an illustration:

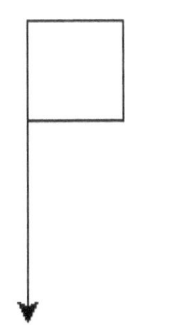

```
>>> t.clear()
>>> |
```

What if we wanted our turtle to do a moonwalk, which is moving backwards while drawing? To get the python turtle to move backwards, we use the backward function(). For example:

```
>>> t.backward(200)
>>> |
```

What if we wanted the turtle to go up or down without making any drawings. What would we do then? First, reset your turtle using the reset function. To make the turtle move up without drawing, we can use the up() function. The up() function makes the turtle move upwards by 30 pixels.

To make the turtle go down without drawing, we use the down() function. This also makes the turtle go down by 30 pixels. If you want to hide the turtle so that you can see what you have created, you can use the hideturtle() function.

Diagrams with straight lines are not the only thing you can create using turtle. To create a circle, we use the circle() function while entering the radius of the circle −the operation of entering values in a function is called parameter passing.

Here is how we create a circle − reset the turtle first before creating a circle:

```
>>> import turtle
>>> t = turtle.Pen()
>>> t.circle(60)
```

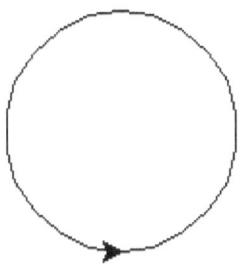

This time, look at the following lines of code and try to guess what they do. If you get them right, Pizza is on me☺.

```
>>> t.reset()
>>> t.color("Green")
>>> t.circle(100)
>>> t.hideturtle()
```

Let us find out what the above lines of code actually do. The first line resets the turtle, the second line sets the color of the turtle to Green, the third creates a circle with a radius of 100, and the third line hides the turtle – I know I owe you a pizza☺.

We change the color of the turtle by simply using the color() function and passing the name of the color we want as the parameter.

We can also fill the drawing we created using the begin_tfill() and end_fill() functions. Let us fill our circle with the color Green.

```
>>> t.begin_fill()
>>> t.circle(100)
>>> t.end_fill()
```

We do not need to pass the color green in the begin_fill() function as we are already using color green – but in case we want another color, we have to enter the color.

NOTE: You MUST end the fill for the filling to be completed. Again, the filling works only if you close your drawing to prevent the color of the drawing from leaking out in the canvas.

Exercise 6

Try out the following exercise:

Question 1

Draw a red rectangle of length 40 pixels and 80 pixels. You should first import the turtle module, create canvas named my_pen, then draw the rectangle, and finally hide the turtle.

Question 2

Write a python program that creates three circles one inside the other. The first circle should have a radius of 60 pixels, the second one should have a radius of 40 pixels, and the last one a radius of 30 pixels. Each circle should have a different color fill from the others.

Question 3

Write a program that creates box that does not have corners as shown below:

Solutions

Let us look at sample solutions for the above questions – you can solve them in any way you find appropriate.

Solution 1

```
>>> import turtle
>>> my_pen = turtle.Pen()
>>> my_pen.color("Red")
>>> my_pen.forward(80)
>>> my_pen.left(90)
>>> my_pen.forward(40)
>>> my_pen.left(90)
>>> my_pen.forward(80)
>>> my_pen.left(90)
>>> my_pen.forward(40)
>>> my_pen.hideturtle()
```

Solution 2

```
>>> import turtle
>>> C = turtle.Pen()
>>> C.fillcolor("blue")
>>> C.begin_fill()
>>> C.circle(60)
>>> C.end_fill()
>>> C.fillcolor("yellow")
>>> C.begin_fill()
>>> C.Circle(40)
Traceback (most recent call last):
  File "<pyshell#8>", line 1, in <module>
    C.Circle(40)
AttributeError: 'Turtle' object has no attribute 'Circle'
>>> C.circle(40)
>>> C.end_fill()
>>> C.fillcolor("red")
>>> C.begin_fill()
>>> C.circle(30)
>>> C.end_fill()
>>> C.hideturtle()
```

Solution 3

```
>>> import turtle
>>> box = turtle.Pen()
>>> box.up()
>>> box.forward(10)
>>> box.down()
>>> box.forward(50)
>>> box.up()
>>> box.forward(10)
>>> box.left(90)
>>> box.forward(10)
>>> box.down()
>>> box.forward(50)
>>> box.up()
>>> box.forward(10)
>>> box.left(90)
>>> box.forward(10)
>>> box.down()
>>> box.forward(50)
>>> box.up()
>>> box.forward(10)
>>> box.left(90)
>>> box.forward(10)
>>> box.down()
>>> box.forward(50)
>>> box.hideturtle()
```

Were you able to work through these exercises on your own? If you did, you are doing amazingly well and are on your way to becoming a Python programming master.

Let us expand your knowledge a bit more by looking at something new:

Part 7: Decision Making

Decision Making in Python

We had a good roll with turtle and drawing items we want it to. What if we wanted to let the turtle decide how many steps to make or in which directions to make these steps?

To perform decisions in Python, we use features known as conditional statements. Before we get to decision making, let us see how we can make our programs interact with the user.

To allow the user to give their input, we use the input function. Can you remember what we did to save our code in case we wanted to reuse it? Here, we are going to look at how to create a new file, edit the code in the file at once, and run it once done —instead of typing line by line as we did previously.

Open the Python IDLE shell and click File – New, and open a new window.

NOTE: For an easy shortcut, use the CRTL + N on Windows or Linux, and Command + N on a Mac.

To use the input function, we simply create the variable we want to ask the user to input and assign it to the input() function. For example, to get the user's name, we type:

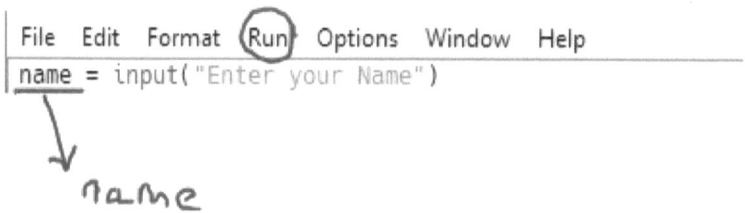

```
File  Edit  Format  Run  Options  Window  Help
name = input("Enter your Name")
```

name

Now save the code by clicking CTRL + S or Command + S on Mac. Now to run the code, click the F5 key.

Once we run the code, it allows us to enter our name and stores it in the variable called name. Now we can use the variable we got from the user. For example, we can print:

```
name = input("Enter your Name: ")
print("%s is such an intelligent kid"%name)

Enter your Name: Ruby
Ruby is such an intelligent kid
```

Now we can use the name the user enters inside the python program. The functionality of interacting with the user makes it more interesting and useful. Now that you know how to create user-interactive programs, let us get back to decision making in Python:

Decision Making in Python

First, let us discuss a conditional statement known as if...statement. The syntax for if statement is —syntax refers to the general/recommended format for doing a certain aspect:

```
if (condition) {

        do some action
```

The condition should be any python expression that is true for the action we intend to perform. For example, we can create a program that asks the user for a first name, if the name is "Ruby" it tells you that you are smart. We can do this by entering the code:

```
name = input("Enter your Name: ")
if (name == "Ruby"):
    print("You are very smart")
```

We can see that once Python takes the input from the user, it stores it in the variable called name. The if statement then examines the value stored in the variable name and compares it to the name "Ruby." If the name matches "Ruby," it performs the action of printing out "You are very smart." Another thing to note is that the action to be performed after an if statement is true is indented inside the if statement.

Note something else too. When we are comparing values with another value, we use two equal signs == rather than the single equal sign =. The double equal sign compares the value of A to the value of B. We use the single equal sign – known as assignment operator— to assign values to variables.

What would happen if we entered another name other than Ruby? This would result to the condition of the if statement being false and the code in the action part would not be run.

```
Enter your Name: Ken
>>> |
```

As you can see, when we provide another name other than "Ruby," nothing happened. You may be wondering to yourself, what would happen if we wanted to do something if the name is not Ruby?

For a case like this, we use another expanded variation of the if...statement called if...else...then statement. Let us modify the code above to do some action if we enter a name that is not Ruby.

```
name = input("Enter your Name: ")
if (name == "Ruby"):
  print("You are very smart")
else:
  print("You should quit that video game")
```

```
Enter your Name: Ken
You should quit that video game
>>>

Enter your Name: Ruby
You are very smart
```

Now we can print "You should quit that video game" if the name entered is not Ruby. However, if it is Ruby, we can also print "You are very smart."

Now let us try decision making with numbers.

How many video games do you play in one day? If the games you play are more than 5, then we print "That is a lot of video games"; otherwise, we print "You need to enjoy the fun of technology".

```python
video_games = input("How many games do you play in one day? ")
video_games = int(video_games)
if (video_games > 5):
  print("That is a lot of video games")
else:
  print("You need to enjoy the fun of technology")
```

Notice what in the second line, we passed the video_games variable to a function called int() in order to convert the user input to a number – this is because Python takes the input from the user as a string. Since Python cannot compare a string with a number. The process of converting a certain data type to another data type is known as type conversion or casting. When we run the program, we get:

```
How many games do you play in one day? 3
You need to enjoy the fun of technology
>>>

How many games do you play in one day? 6
That is a lot of video games
```

In most cases, in the condition part of conditional statements, we perform a comparison between values. The most common type of comparison you can perform in Python includes the following:

Comparison Symbol	Comparison definition
==	Equal to
>	Greater than
<	Less than
>=	Greater than or equal to
<=	Less than or equal to
!=	Not equal to

Let us move on to another important aspect. Here is a question:

What if we wanted to perform an action if your name is Ruby, another action if your name is Ken, another action if your name is Potter, and another action if your name is any other apart from the three? To do this, we use the the elif feature in Python

Check out this example below:

```python
name = input("Provide your name please: ")
if (name == "Ruby"):
  print("You are very Smart")
elif (name == "Ken"):
  print("You should quit that video game")
elif(name == "Potter"):
  print("Lord Voldemort is Coming for You")
else:
  print("You do not belong to our group")
```

```
Provide your name please: Potter
Lord Voldemort is Coming for You
>>>

Provide your name please: Ruby
You are very Smart
>>>

Provide your name please: Ken
You should quit that video game
>>>

Provide your name please: Robert
You do not belong to our group
```

The elif condition is a short form of the else..if – it checks if a condition is true and if not, it moves to the next condition until a condition evaluates to true. If we run the program and provide a different input everytime, we get a different output. We can have as many elif statements as we want – this aspect of more than one elif statement is what we call nested conditions.

Let us move on to the next aspect. Here is another question for you:

What would we do if we wanted to check if a condition is true more than once? For example, if we ask a user to provide his/her name and check the condition as If name is Ruby or Ken then print "Welcome to our friend's group." We can combine these conditions using logical operators. For example:

```
name = input("Enter your name: ")
if (name == "Ruby" or name == "Ken"):
    print("Welcome to the the friend's gruop")
elif(name == "Emma" or name == "Potter"):
    print("Thank you for being my friends")
else:
    print("You are not my friend")
```

```
Enter your name: Ken
Welcome to the the friend's gruop
```

Once the user provides the name, python checks if the name is either Ruby or Ken, and if true, it runs the first block of code, else if the name is Emma or Potter, run the second block of code and finally, if its neither, run the third block of code.

Apart from the OR operator, there are other logical operators. We can also use the AND operator. For example, if we want the age of 1 to 3 years to be a child and between 5 to 12 to be kid, we use the and operator in Python. As shown below:

```python
age = input("Enter your age: ")
age = int(age)
if (age <= 3):
    print("You are a child")
elif(age>=5 and age<=12):
    print("You are a kid")
else:
    print("You are an adult")
```

If we run the above code and provide different ages, each age will have a different output.

```
Enter your age: 3
You are an adult
>>>
=========== RESTART: C:/Users/capta/OneDrive/Documents/class.py ===========
Enter your age: 3
You are a child
>>>
=========== RESTART: C:/Users/capta/OneDrive/Documents/class.py ===========
Enter your age: 7
You are a kid
>>>
=========== RESTART: C:/Users/capta/OneDrive/Documents/class.py ===========
Enter your age: 15
You are an adult
```

That covers the section of decision making. The exercise below will test out your knowledge:

Exercise 7

Here goes:

Question 1

Write a program that asks the user for a username and password. If the username and password are correct, the program prints "Access Granted." If either the username or the password is wrong, print "Access Denied".

Question 2

Write a program that grades the student's performance according to their provided marks. The ranking should be as follows

❖ 95 – 100 – Excellent

❖ 75 – 94 – Very Good

❖ 55 -74 – Good

❖ 45 – 54 – Satisfactory

❖ Below 45 – Work Harder

Question 3

Write a python program that asks the user if they want to draw a circle or a square, if the input is circle, ask for the radius of the circle and if the input is square, ask for the side of the rectangle and then draw the provided input.

Solutions

Solution 1

```python
username = input("Enter your username: ")
password = input("Enter the password: ")
if username == "Admin" and password = "password":
    print("Access Granted")
else:
    print("Access Denied")
```

Solution 2

```python
score = input("Enter the student score")
score = int(score)
if score >= 95:
    print("Excellent")
elif socre >= 75:
    print("Very Good")
elif score >= 55:
    print("Good")
elif score >= 45:
    print("Satisfactory")
elif socre <= 44:
    print("Work Harder")
else:
    print("Out of range")
```

Solution 3

```
import turtle
figure = turtle.Pen()
draw = input("Square or Cicrle")
if draw == "Square":
    size = input("Enter the size of the square")
    size = int(size)
    figure.forward(size)
    figure.left(90)
    figure.forward(size)
    figure.left(90)
    figure.forward(size)
    figure.left(90)
    figure.forward(size)
    figure.left(90)
elif draw = "Circle":
    size = input("Enter the radius of the circle")
    size = int(size)
    figure.circle(size)
else:
    print("Incorrect Choice")
```

Part 8: Loops – Control Flow

How to Work With Loops in Python

If you practice with the python turtle module, you will, at times, notice that you must repeat the same code several times when drawing certain shapes. There is a way to solve this kind of repetitive actions in Python. That is the topic for this section.

When it comes to repetitive actions in a program, it is always a best practice to use loops. Let us use a simple example to illustrate this. If we want to print the word hello 5 times, we can just write `print("Hello")` 5 times. What if we wanted to print the word hello 1000 times, how would we do that when copying and pasting one line of code would be very tiresome?

Let us see a simpler way to print the word Hello World 5 times. Look carefully at the code below:

```
>>> for x in range(0,5):
        print("Hello world")


Hello world
Hello world
Hello world
Hello world
Hello world
```

Let us see what is happening in this line of code.

In the first line, we create a variable called x and set the value to 0 – this is the first number within the parenthesis. It also checks whether the value of x is within the range of 0 and 5. If the check is true, it prints the word "Hello world."

Next, each time python prints the string on the screen, it automatically updates the value of x by 1 and runs the check again. Look at the illustration below:

Round	check value	condition
1	0	True
2	1	True
3	2	True
4	3	True
5	4	True
6	5	false

In the first run, the value is 0 and since 0 is less than 5, it prints the hello world first time. It then automatically updates the value of 0 by adding 1. It then checks if 1 is less than 5, which evaluates to true. This continues until it reaches to 5. Since 5 is not less 5, the loop stops automatically.

We call each round of a loop an *iteration*. Let us modify the program to see the value of x on each iteration.

```
>>> for x in range(0,5):
        print("The value of x is %s"%x)


The value of x is 0
The value of x is 1
The value of x is 2
The value of x is 3
The value of x is 4
```

Now let us try running the loop to print "Hello world" 1000 times. Try it by yourself; you just need to modify the value to 1000.

```
>>> for x in range(0,1000):
        print("Hello world %s"%x)
```

```
Hello world 988
Hello world 989
Hello world 990
Hello world 991
Hello world 992
Hello world 993
Hello world 994
Hello world 995
Hello world 996
Hello world 997
Hello world 998
Hello world 999
```

As much fun as it is to print a loop many times, loops have very important applications when it comes to complex applications. In fact, a common jibe in the programming world is that if you can write loops well, you are a great programmer.

Loops can also work with lists, tuples, and even dictionaries. Can you remember the list we created containing friend's names and ages? When printing the list of friends, we used print(my_friends). However, the format was not very pleasing. We can use loops to modify the output and add some additional information. Check the example below:

```
>>> my_friends = ["Robert","Riley","Hermione","James","Ann"]
>>> for x in my_friends:
        print("%s is my friend"%x)


Robert is my friend
Riley is my friend
Hermione is my friend
James is my friend
Ann is my friend
```

In this case, the for loop is somehow different. You may notice that it does not contain an in range() function but instead, we provided the name of the list. This time, the value x —referred to as a counter— takes the value of the items in the provided list. The counter is dynamic such that if the list contains string values, x is string and if the list contains a number, x is a number.

However, the counter does not necessarily have the name x — you can call it whatever name you want— just be creative and meaningful. Can you remember the instance when we wanted to calculate the age of each friend after 15 years? For that case, we had to use the print statement for each friend. Now that we know about loops, we can make this task easier. Similar to the if statements, you can have an entire block of code inside a for loop.

Let us try to make slight adjustment to our previous code to print the age of our friends in 10 years.

```
>>> my_friends = ["Robert","Riley","Hermione","James","Ann"]
>>> ages = [15,12,10,11,16]
>>> for x in range(0,5):
        print("%s is my friend"%my_friends[x])
        print("%s will be %s years old in 10 yrs"%(my_friends[x], ages[x] + 10))


Robert is my friend
Robert will be 25 years old in 10 yrs
Riley is my friend
Riley will be 22 years old in 10 yrs
Hermione is my friend
Hermione will be 20 years old in 10 yrs
James is my friend
James will be 21 years old in 10 yrs
Ann is my friend
Ann will be 26 years old in 10 yrs
```

For the situation above, we cannot pass one list as the counter variable since we need information from both lists. Again, since we want information for all friends in the list, we set the range to 5.

Let us check out the use of for loops with dictionaries. For example:

```
>>> my_friends = {"Robert":15,"Riley":12,"Hermione":10,"James":11,"Ann":16}
>>> for x in my_friends:
        print("%s is %s years old"%(x, my_friends[x]))


Robert is 15 years old
Riley is 12 years old
Hermione is 10 years old
James is 11 years old
Ann is 16 years old
```

In this way, even if we had a list of 1000 friends to work with, we would easily accomplish this task using simple lines of code.

What if you had 1000 dollars in your account —or under the bed☺— and each day, you withdraw certain amount of money. For how many days would you use the money?

Well, first you would have to know the amount of money you use each day, how often you withdraw, what if you withdraw more on some days than you do on other days –approaching certain problems presents many questions. Luckily, Python provides another loop known as a while loop.

A while loop is not that much different from the for loop except for a small difference. A for loop repeats a loop – performs an operation for a known number of times. For example, you only need to print information for 5 of your friends etc. On the other hand, A while loop, is responsible for repeating a given block of code as long as the condition is true or false. A simpler way to think of it is a loop with an if statement inside. Let us solve the money problem using a while loop. Look carefully at the code below and try to analyze what it does.

```python
account_balance = 1000
while account_balance != 0:
    withdraw = input("Enter the amount to withdraw today: ")
    withdraw = int(withdraw)
    account_balance = account_balance - withdraw
    print("Your account balance is %s"%account_balance)

print("Error, Account balance is 0")
```

Did you find out what the loop does?

First, we create a variable with account balance as 1000. Next, python checks if the account balance is 0. If not, we ask the user for the amount to withdraw —we have to convert this to a number since the input is a string. Next, we update the account balance by subtracting the withdrawn amount from the account balance. Then we tell the user how much money is in the account after a withdrawal. Finally, if the user account balance runs out —thus the condition turns false— we alert the user.

Let us see an example:

```
Enter the amount to withdraw today: 100
Your account balance is 900
Enter the amount to withdraw today: 500
Your account balance is 400
Enter the amount to withdraw today: 300
Your account balance is 100
Enter the amount to withdraw today: 100
Your account balance is 0
Error, Account balance is 0
```

The ilustration below gives detailed information about the loop execution:

Iteration Number	money_withdrawn	money_in_bank	money_in_bank != 0	Execute Loop?
0		$1000	True	Yes
1	$100	$900	True	Yes
2	$500	$400	True	Yes
3	$300	$100	True	Yes
4	$100	$0	False	No

Think of something like an instance where someone enters a number larger than the value of the account balance. This would result in a loop that never ends. In programming, the scenario of a loop that never ends is known as an infinite loop. To solve a case like this, we introduce a statement called break.

Let us see more.

```python
account_balance = 1000
while account_balance != 0:
    withdraw = input("Enter the amount to withdraw today: ")
    withdraw = int(withdraw)
    account_balance = account_balance - withdraw
    if withdraw > account_balance:
        break
    print("Your account balance is %s"%account_balance)
print("Error, Account balance is 0")
```

```
Enter the amount to withdraw today: 120
Your account balance is 880
Enter the amount to withdraw today: 100
Your account balance is 780
Enter the amount to withdraw today: 8990
Error, Account balance is 0
```

If you enter an amount larger than the balance, Python will automatically stop the loop.

That is all there is to learn about loops

Exercise 8

Use this exercise to test out what you have learned thus far:

Question 1

Write a python program that asks a user for a name input and printouts the name 150 times filling up the screen:

Question 2:

Let us do some math:

Write a python program that allows the user to enter a number. The program should then print all the even numbers from 2 up to that number. If the number is 0, alert the user "Error number has to be more than."

HINT: A number is even if it is divisible by 2 without a remainder.

Question 3

Use python turtle and loops to create a program that prints out the following picture.

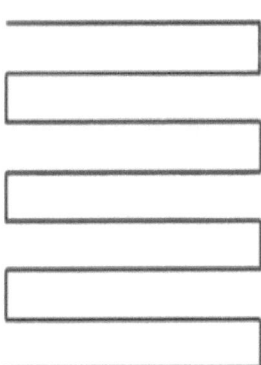

Were you able to solve these exercise questions?

Great job! You are doing amazingly well thus far. Let us build on what you have learned by introducing something new:

Solution 1

```
name = input("Enter your name: ")
for i in range(0, 151):
    print(name, end="")
```

Solution 2

```
number = input("Enter a number")
number = int(number)
if number == 0:
    print("Error number needs to more than 0")
else:
    for i in range(2, number):
        return number % 2 == 0
```

Solution 3

```
import turtle
t = turtle.Pen()
for i in range(0, 5):
    t.forward(90)
    f.left(90)
    t.forward(50)
    t.left(90)
```

Part 9: Functions

Working with Python Functions

In this section, we are going to learn a very important programming technique known as Reduce, Reuse, and Recycle that falls under the category of functions in programming.

Loops are very effective if we are repeating an action many times over. However, if we want to repeat lines of code, we must use functions. A function is a block of code that contains other code within it to perform a task. We have used functions before.

In the background, without functions, we would have to enter a code like this every time we need to print out something on the screen:

```
import collections as _collections
import re
import sys as _sys
import types as _types
from io import StringIO as _StringIO

__all__ = ["pprint","pformat","isreadable","isrecursive","saferepr",
           "PrettyPrinter"]


def pprint(object, stream=None, indent=1, width=80, depth=None, *,
           compact=False):
    """Pretty-print a Python object to a stream [default is sys.stdout]."""
    printer = PrettyPrinter(
        stream=stream, indent=indent, width=width, depth=depth,
        compact=compact)
    printer.pprint(object)

def pformat(object, indent=1, width=80, depth=None, *, compact=False):
    """Format a Python object into a pretty-printed representation."""
    return PrettyPrinter(indent=indent, width=width, depth=depth,
                         compact=compact).pformat(object)

def saferepr(object):
    """Version of repr() which can handle recursive data structures."""
    return _safe_repr(object, {}, None, 0)[0]

def isreadable(object):
    """Determine if saferepr(object) is readable by eval()."""
    return _safe_repr(object, {}, None, 0)[1]

def isrecursive(object):
    """Determine if object requires a recursive representation."""
    return _safe_repr(object, {}, None, 0)[2]

class _safe_key:
    """Helper function for key functions when sorting unorderable objects.

    The wrapped-object will fallback to a Py2.x style comparison for
    unorderable types (sorting first comparing the type name and then by
    the obj ids).  Does not work recursively, so dict.items() must have
    _safe_key applied to both the key and the value.

    """

    __slots__ = ['obj']

    def __init__(self, obj):
```

Once we create a function, we can then use it to perform the specified task whenever needed. Let us look at an example.

If you wanted to create a code for a rectangle and then create 10 other rectangles, you would have to type the code 10 times. The aspect of repeating code is not a fun part of programming.

For the rectangle problem, we can create a function that contains the code for creating the desired rectangle. We can then call the function to create the rectangle as many times as we want.

Example of functions that we already used include: print(), list(), range() —that is why they were using parenthesis. However, the functions we used were built-in functions, meaning they come preinstalled in Python. We can also create our own functions to reuse.

To create a function, we must understand its syntax. A python function has three key components. They include:

❖ a name

❖ function parameters

❖ function body

These three components work together as follows:

```
def function_name(parameters):

    function_body
```

The function structure is similar to the structure of the for and while loops. You must indent the function body. The function name can be any name you like as long it follows the rules on naming a variable that we discussed earlier in the variable section.

The next part is the parameters. Parameters are the variables that the function will be taking to perform its specific task. For example, in the print function, we passed either the number, a string, or a variable to print out. Parameters are not always required and you can create a function without parameters.

The function body contains the lines of code that define what the function does. For example, if you have a program that tests the maximum and minimum value between two numbers, you will write the code to test out this problem inside the function body.

Whenever you need to use a function, you just call the function using its name. If the function requires parameters, you MUST pass these parameters during the function call.

Let us see an example that prints out the "Hello, I am your first function"

```
def print_me():
    print("I am your first function")
print_me()
```

Note that this is a function without parameters and thus, we did not need to pass them during the function call. Now we can use this function whenever we need it in the entire program.

Here are some of the reasons why functions are important:

❖ Simplifies the process of coding

❖ Allows for code reuse

❖ It makes debugging a lot easier —debugging is the process of finding and fixing errors in a program

❖ It reduces the code size and makes it clean and readable

Let us now see how to work with a function that has parameters. Use the max and min functions.

```
>>> def min_max(number1, number2):
        if (number1 > number2):
                print("Max number is %s"%number1)
        else:
                print("Maximum number is %s"%number2)


>>> min_max(10,20)
Maximum number is 20
```

Above, we declared a function called min_max that takes two arguments: number1 and number2. The function checks if the first number is greater than the second number. If it is, the maximum number is the first number; otherwise, the maximum number is the second number. During the function call, we passed in the numbers we wanted to test — in this case 10 and 20. The program then checks for the maximum and returns the value.

If you want to create a function that you can use across all your python programs, we create a file that contains the function code and then import it in other files.

Can you remember the toy business project we worked on earlier? We can create a python function to calculate the amount earned in one day. The parameters required are total number of toys, toys spoilt, and the cost of each toy. Create a new file and save it, making sure you remember the name of the file as well as the function name.

```
def income_per_day(total_toys, toys_spoilt, cost_per_toy):
    total_money = (total_toys - toys_spoilt) * cost
    print("Total income = %S" %total_money)
```

To use the function in another file, simply create a new file and use the import module.

```
from daily_income import income_per_day
cost_per_toy = 25
day1_total = input("Enter the total number of toys in that day: ")
day1_total = int(day1_total)
day1_spoilt = input("How many toys were spoilt: ")
day1_spoilt = int(day1_spoilt)
print("Day 1 result: ")

# function call
income_per_day(day1_total, day1_spoilt, cost_per_toy)
```

```
Enter the total number of toys in that day: 200
How many toys were spoilt: 10
Day 1 result:
Total income = 4750
```

Now we can use the income_per_day function in all the required programs. All we have to do is change the required arguments.

Variables created within a function are only visible within a function. For example, if you try to use the variable such as total_money in the main program, it will result in an error. This aspect of variable accessibility is what we refer to as a variable or function scope. Therefore, the variable such as total_money has a scope of its created function. This means that once the function executes, the attendant results is the immediate destruction of the variable.

If you want to use the result of a function call, we use the keyword return followed by the value we want returned. When Python comes across the return keyword in a function, it knows that it has come to the end of the function and returns the current value from the function call. However, you can only return one value from a function. The return keyword also indicates the end of the function execution and any code beyond the return keyword will not execute.

Let us test out your understanding of the various principles learned in this part of this python guidebook:

Exercise 9

Question 1

Write a python function that asks the user for a name input and the number of times to print the name. Use loops to solve this problem.

Question 2

Expand the toy business program we worked with earlier to calculate the income for five consecutive days —use loops.

Question 3

Write a python program that creates a rectangle using the python turtle module. Use the rectangle function to draw a bookshelf.

Now that we have had tons of practice writing python code and programs, we need to look at another important feature, a feature that you must master before you can master programming —in Python and in other programming languages:

Solution 1

```python
def name(name, times):
    name = input("Enter your name: ")
    times = input("Enter the number of times: ")
    times = int(times)
    for in range(0, times):
        print(name)
name()
```

Solution 3

```python
import turtle
t = turtle.Pen()
def rectange():
    t.forward(100)
    t.left(90)
    t.forward(50)
    t.left(90)
    t.forward(100)
    t.left(90)
    t.forward(50)
for i in range(0, 10):
    rectange()
```

Part 10: Finding and Fixing Bugs

How to Debug your Python Programs

In this section, we are going to learn another important skill. We are going to find and fix errors in a program. In programming, we call Errors 'bugs,' which makes the process of finding and fixing them 'debugging.' According to many programmers, debugging is the hardest part of programming.

If there is a problem with your code, Python will help you out by displaying an error message. For beginners, these errors do not make much sense and trying to fix them may lead to more bugs. In Python, both the IDLE editor and the shell will display these error messages.

In Python, Error messages always appear in red text and the program execution may stop once it encounters an error. To determine what the error message is indicating, the best practice is to understand the different types of errors in Python as well as their primary causes.

The following are the most common types of python errors and their main causes.

Syntax Errors

As we had previously discussed, if you encounter a syntax error, it indicates you have typed something incorrectly. If this happens, Python indicates the file and the line of code containing the error.

When Python indicates a syntax error, look out for the following issues:

❖ Matching opening and closing brackets

❖ Missing quotation marks

❖ Misspelled words and python syntax

The illustration below shows a missing quotation mark

```
>>> print(hello world")
SyntaxError: invalid syntax
```

Typed Errors

In Python, typed errors indicate mixed data types such as mixing numbers with strings. Confusing data types is like using a hammer to shovel sand or trying to use the fridge to bake a cake.

```
>>> total_amount = "50" + 50
Traceback (most recent call last):
  File "<pyshell#1>", line 1, in <module>
    total_amount = "50" + 50
TypeError: can only concatenate str (not "int") to str
```

In the above example, the first "50" is a string type while the second is a number type. Since you cannot add a number and string, Python provides a type error as shown in line 5

Indentation Errors

Python utilizes indentation to understand where a block of code is. For example, the function and the loop body were indented. Indentation errors occur when we have a compromised code structure and Python does not understand the code. We must correctly indent the next line after the colon ():

To indent the code, you can press tab once or space four times. Failing to indent code that needs indenting appears as a syntax error in Python:

```
>>> if (name == "Ruby"):
print("Hello Ruby")
SyntaxError: expected an indented block
```

Name Errors

A name error occurs when using variable names of undeclared variables. Since Python is case-sensitive, a single typo will result in an error. To avoid name errors, always declare variables before writing the code to use them.

```
>>> print("My first name is: %s"%first_name)
Traceback (most recent call last):
  File "<pyshell#3>", line 1, in <module>
    print("My first name is: %s"%first_name)
NameError: name 'first_name' is not defined
```

Logical Errors

Logical errors are the most difficult to find and fix. Logical errors do not result in an error; instead, the program does not work as expected. For example, the toy problem resulted in a logical error since the price was even lower than the total number of toys. If your program is not working correctly but it cannot detect the problem or display the error, create a new program and edit the code line by line running it before adding new code.

Finding and fixing bugs can be the most disappointing part of programming as you may spend hours trying to find and fix an error.

Here are some questions to consider when fixing bugs:

❖ What changes have I done since the last successful run?

❖ Have I mixed lower case and upper-case letters?

❖ Do all closing and opening brackets match? For example, [], (), {} etc.

❖ Have I spelled everything correctly?

If you keep these principles in mind, you should be able to find and fix errors or bugs that may be keeping your Python program from running effectively.

At this point in the guide, we have learned tons about python programming. In the next section of the guide, we shall work on an interactive project that combines most of what you have learned in this guidebook thus far:

Part 11: Step-by-Step Python Project

In this section, we are going to create fun project using the python turtle graphics. In this project, we are going to create a circle loop to create a 2d circle

Step 1

The first step is to create a file and name it circle_shape.py.

Step 2

Next, import the turtle module and create a turtle pen called turtle_circle.

Step 3

Draw a shape as turtle.

Step 4

Create a for loop with range of 60 and set the loop body to create a circle with a radius of iterator * 3. Add direction as left on 10 points

Final code and diagram

```
>>> import turtle
>>> turtle_circle = turtle.Pen()
>>> turtle_circle.shape("turtle")
>>> turtle.speed(5)
>>> for x in range(60):
        turtle_circle(x*3)
        gordon.right(10)
>>> for x in range(60):
        turtle_circle.circle(x*3)
        turtle_circle.right(10)
```

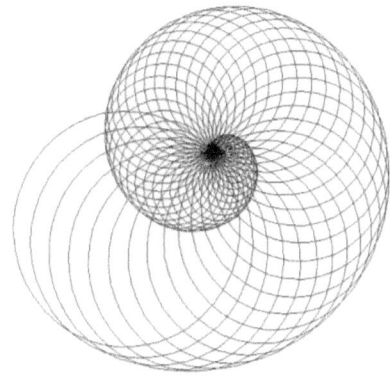

Conclusion

Thank you for reading this guide!

As you may have noted, learning how to program in Python is relatively easy and fun. To master the various python elements we have discussed in this guide, the most important thing you need to do is practice coding every chance you get. The more you write code, the better you shall become, and the easier it shall become to master python programming.

If you found the book valuable, can you recommend it to others? One way to do that is to post a review on Amazon.

Please leave a review for this book on Amazon by visiting the page below:

https://amzn.to/2VMR5qr

Your Gift

Let me help you master this and other programming languages quickly.

Visit

https://bit.ly/codetutorials

To Find Out More